Bible Stories GONE CRAZY!

by Josh Edwards

Illustrated by
Emiliano Migliardo

CANDLE
BOOKS

Published by Candle Books
an imprint of
Lion Hudson plc
Wilkinson House, Jordan Hill Road,
Oxford OX2 8DR, England
www.lionhudson.com/candle

ISBN 978 1 78128 190 1

First edition 2015

A catalogue record for this book is available from the British Library

Printed and bound in Poland,
February 2016, LH44

Bible Stories Gone Crazy!

Emiliano the artist has put lots of
funny mistakes into his drawings.
See how many you can find on each page.

Use the Bible verses to look up each story
and help you answer some of the questions.

Can you spot Teddy  in every picture?
Sometimes he appears more than once!

Noah and his Great Ark

"I'm going to send a great flood," God told Noah. "Build a huge ark and fill it with two of every animal. I will save them *all* from the flood that's coming." So Noah and his three sons got busy building an enormous ark.

Genesis 6:9–22

Do you think Noah really painted the ark?

Did Noah have glass windows in the ark?

How many pairs of animals are there?

How many workmen are taking a break?

Did Noah have electric tools and cement mixers?

Can you find Noah? Who helped him build the ark?

How many workmen are eating sandwiches?

Which workman do you think is having the most fun?

How many different birds can you find?

Which animal doesn't have a mate?

Moses and the Miracle Escape

Moses' people, the Israelites, lived as slaves in Egypt. God told Moses to help them escape. But the king of Egypt chased them all the way to the Red Sea. Then God opened up a path through the water.

How many Egyptians are carrying spears?

Why have the Israelites got so much luggage?

What's happened to the man putting up a windbreak?

Do you know what happened to the Egyptian soldiers? Did they catch the Israelites?

Can you find Moses? What's he carrying?

Can you find Egyptians riding anything that hadn't yet been invented?

Did the Israelites really have surfboards?

What has the fisherman caught?

What animals are the Israelites taking with them?

What's happening to the lifeguard?

Joshua Destroys Jericho

God told Joshua to march his people around the city of Jericho for seven days. Priests carried the Holy Ark. On the seventh day they blew ram's horn trumpets and shouted very loud. The walls collapsed – and the city fell!

Joshua 6:1–20

What is the wolf trying to do?

What happened after the priests blew their trumpets?

What other animals can you find – besides the wolf?

Which bricks don't belong in the old city of Jericho? Why?

Who was the leader of God's people?

Can you find a soldier with a peculiar weapon?

Which priest is knocking down the walls in a crazy way?

What are the four priests carrying?

Did a rock band really play when the walls fell down?

Little David Beats Goliath

Young David the shepherd killed the bully Goliath with just one stone thrown from his sling. Goliath's army ran away as soon as he fell.

1 Samuel 17

How many swords can you find?

Where did the stone hit Goliath?

Do you know what Goliath's people were called?

What ball games can you see? Did people play them in David's time?

Which army does the parachutist belong to?

Can you find someone who has missed the fight?

Do you know the name of the king of Israel at this time?

Did they have planes in David's time?

What are the scouts cooking on their campfire?

Daniel in the Pit of Lions

The king threw Daniel into a pit full of hungry lions. Daniel prayed hard – and God sent an angel to shut the lions' mouths. The king was amazed!

Daniel 6:1–28

How many lions are in the pit?

What different things are the lions doing?

What is this angel carrying?

Do you know why the king threw Daniel into the pit of lions?

When did you last see a lion?

Do you know what happened next to Daniel?

What game is the lion near the door playing?

Which lion do you think is the funniest?

How many balloons are in the picture?

Jonah and the Monster Fish

Some sailors threw poor Jonah into the stormy sea. But God sent a ginormous fish to swallow him up. After three days, the fish spat him out safely on the seashore.

How many different land animals can you find?

Can you find a flying carpet?

Why is the man with a megaphone shouting?

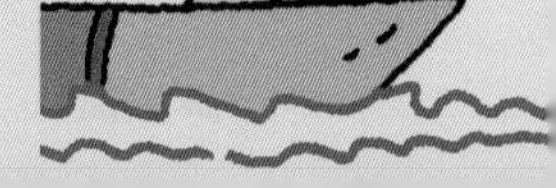

Can you find anyone having a picnic in a strange place?

Can you find a mermaid? What is she doing?

How many sailors – modern and old – are in the picture?

Can you find a golfer? Where is he standing?

Can you find a boat from Venice? Do you know what these boats are called?

What did Jonah do next?

Jesus Feeds a Huge Crowd

Jesus talked to these people all day, till they grew very hungry.
A boy gave Jesus his lunch - five loaves and two fish.
By a miracle, Jesus fed everyone with that one boy's meal.

John 6:1–14

How many baskets can you find?

Can you find three people sharing a sandwich?

Do you know the name of the lake?

Who gave Jesus his lunch?

How many babies can you find?

Who's stealing a fish?

Can you find a waiter? Is he wearing clothes from Bible times?

Who's not eating loaves and fishes?

Who's getting lunch at a ride-thru?

Man Through the Roof!

One day Jesus was talking in a crowded house. Four men took their sick friend on the roof, made a hole, and lowered him down. Jesus healed him! The man jumped up and thanked God.

Mark 2:1–12

What's the funniest thing in this picture?

Can you find anyone sunbathing?

Can you find a man singing a love song?

Why did the sick man's friends make a hole in the roof?

Can you find a Mexican band singing?

What are the cowboys doing?

What happened to the man who Jesus healed?

How many different sorts of hat can you find?

What is this man trying to pull?

Where's the tight-rope walker?

Did you find all the teddies?

THE TEDDY TALLY

Noah and his Great Ark
3 teddies

Moses and the Miracle Escape
2 teddies

Joshua Destroys Jericho
2 teddies

Little David Beats Goliath
2 teddies

Daniel in the Pit of Lions
2 teddies

Jonah and the Monster Fish
1 teddy

Jesus Feeds a Huge Crowd
2 teddies

Man Through the Roof
2 teddies